I0178844

Anonymous

More Maritime Melodies

A collection of poems and ballads of the sea, together with an appendix,

not poetical but wordly wise

Anonymous

More Maritime Melodies
A collection of poems and ballads of the sea, together with an appendix, not poetical but wordly wise

ISBN/EAN: 9783744797450

Printed in Europe, USA, Canada, Australia, Japan

Cover: Foto ©Thomas Meinert / pixelio.de

More available books at **www.hansebooks.com**

MORE

MARITIME MELODIES

—A COLLECTION OF—

*Poems and Ballads of the Sea, together with
an Appendix, both Poetical and Worldly-wise.*

✻

COMPLIMENTS OF THE

Commercial Publishing Company

—WITH—

A MERRY CHRISTMAS

—AND—

A HAPPY NEW YEAR

TO EACH READER.

✻

✱ ✱ Preface ✱ ✱

TO FIRST EDITION.

"For lucky rhymes to him were scrip and share,
And mellow metres more than cent for cent."

IN PRESENTING this little volume to its friends, the COMMERCIAL PUBLISHING COMPANY has a two-fold object. It desires to offer its patrons at this season of good will a slight token of its appreciation of many past favors, and incidentally to give its friends an opportunity of seeing a specimen of the good work its presses are capable of.

The Company, an outgrowth of consolidation of the COMMERCIAL NEWS with the business of its former printers, feels that its prosperity is in a large measure due to the warm friendship and liberal patronage of those "that go down to the sea in ships, that do business in great waters;" of the owners, charterers, insurers of vessel property, and merchants identified with shipping and kindred interests. The selection of poems with the sea for their subject seems therefore most appropriate. Trusting the readers of this volume will gain a half hour's recreation from perusing its pages and with the best wishes for a prosperous new year, we remain

Very truly yours,

THE COMMERCIAL PUBLISHING Co.

Christmas, 1889.

✳ ✳ Preface ✳ ✳

TO SECOND EDITION.

"For lucky shares and scrip came from the rhymes,
And cent for cent from mellow metres came."

THUS is Tennyson reversed, and for good reason. In 1889, as a Christmas greeting to the friends of the COMMERCIAL NEWS and the COMMERCIAL PUBLISHING COMPANY, Maritime Melodies, edition 1,000 copies, was launched. The demand exceeded the supply, as is usually the case when good things are given away, and this Christmas a new edition, entirely changed, and it is hoped, improved, is put forth, and a copy sent you with the compliments of the season.

Meanwhile, since the issue of the 1889 edition, the facilities of the COMMERCIAL PUBLISHING COMPANY for executing high class work in its line have been materially increased, the reputation of the COMMERCIAL NEWS for accuracy and honesty has been preserved and in the lustre of added years of faithful service it now shines forth to illumine the path of the merchant and the course of the navigator.

In the hope of finding an excuse for another edition we remain

Very truly yours,

THE COMMERCIAL PUBLISHING Co.

Christmas, 1894.

The Sea.

DAWN is dim on the dark soft water,
  Soft and passionate, dark and sweet;
Love's own self was the deep sea's daughter,
  Fair and flawless from face to feet;
Hailed of all when the world was golden,
Loved of all lovers whose names beholden
Thrill men's eyes as with light of olden
  Days more glad than their flight was fleet.

So they sang; but for men that love her,
  Souls that hear not her word in vain.
Earth beside her and heaven above her
  Seem but shadows that wax and wane.
Softer than sleep's are the sea's caresses,
Kinder than love's that betrays and blesses.
Blither than spring's when her flowerful tresses
  Shake forth sunlight and shine with rain.

All the strength of the waves that perish
  Swells beneath me and laughs and sighs,
Sighs for love of the life they cherish.
  Laughs to know that it lives and dies;
Dies for joy of its life, and lives,
Thrilled with joy that its brief death gives,
Death whose laugh or whose breath forgives
  Change that bids it subside and rise.

                    —*Algernon Charles Swinburne.*

Ben Bolt.

[The song "Ben Bolt" might almost be said to be one of the features
in Du Maurier's "Trilby." It is the song which the heroine of that
much-read story sings so abominably at the beginning of the book,
and so divinely toward the close of it, but which a little later on she
sings in her old manner again and is accordingly hooted off the stage
in London. It seems that, in 1843, Dr. Thomas Dunn English (now a
member of Congress from New Jersey) was asked by N. P. Willis to
write a sea song for the "New Mirror," which Willis and George P.
Morris had just galvanized into life from the corpse of the New York
"Mirror." In 1846, a hanger-on of the Pittsburg Theatre gave one
Nelson F. Kneass a garbled version of the words of the song, which
he had found in an English newspaper, and Kneass set the thing to
music and sang it in a play called "The Battle of Buena Vista." The
piece traveled with him all over the country, "was picked up by all
the minstrel troupes, went to Australia and the Sandwich Isles and
wherever the English language was spoken, was sung in London, and
had all kinds of parodies and replies among the street ballads of that
city." It is said that sixty thousand copies of the music were sold by
Peters. Half a dozen other settings were published, but none of them
had the popularity of Kneass's air, which was adapted from a German
melody, the original of which was afterward published with the same
words. The song has had as many claimants as "Beautiful Snow."
It is odd that the poem should have made such a tremendous sensa-
tion in its day, for the verse is by no means good, and the sentiment
is hackneyed and commonplace.]

DON'T you remember sweet Alice, Ben Bolt—
  Sweet Alice, whose hair was so brown,
Who wept with delight when you gave her a smile,
  And trembled with fear at your frown?
In the old church-yard in the valley, Ben Bolt,
  In a corner obscure and alone,
They have fitted a slab of the granite so gray,
  And Alice lies under the stone.

Under the hickory tree, Ben Bolt,
  Which stood at the foot of the hill,
Together we've lain in the noonday shade,
  And listened to Appleton's mill.
The mill wheel has fallen to pieces, Ben Bolt,

The rafters have tumbled in,
And a quiet which crawls round the walls as you gaze,
  Has followed the olden din.

Do you mind the cabin of logs, Ben Bolt,
  At the edge of the pathless wood,
And the button-ball tree, with its motley limbs,
  Which nigh by the doorstep stood?˙
The cabin to ruin has gone, Ben Bolt,
  The tree you would seek for in vain;
And where once the lords of the forest waived
  Are grass and golden grain.

And don't you remember the school, Ben Bolt,
  With the master so cruel and grim,
And the shaded nook in the running brook
  Where the children went to swim?
Grass grows on the master's grave, Ben Bolt,
  The spring of the brook is dry,
And of all the boys who went to school,
  There are only you and I.

There is a change in the things I loved, Ben Bolt,
  They have changed from the old to the new;
But I feel in the depths of my spirit the truth,
  There never was change in you.
Twelvemonths twenty have past, Ben Bolt,
  Since first we were friends—yet I hail
Your presence a blessing, your friendship a truth,
  Ben Bolt of the salt sea gale.
                    —*Thomas Dunn English.*

The Sea King.

FROM out his castle on the sand
He lead his tawny-bearded band
In stormy bark from land to land.

The red dawn was his goodly sign,
He set his face to sleet and brine,
And quaffed the blast like ruddy wine.

And often felt the swirling gale
Beat, like some giant thresher's flail,
Upon his battered coat of mail;

Or sacked, at times, some windy town,
And from the pastures, parched and brown,
He drove the scurrying cattle down;

And kissed the maids, and stole the bell
From off the church below the fell,
And drowned the priest within the well.

And he had seen, on frosty nights,
Strange, whirling forms and elfin sights,
In twilight land, by Northern Lights;

Or, sailing on by windless shoal,
Had heard, by night, the song of troll
Within some cavern-haunted knoll.

Off Iceland, too, the sudden rush
Of waters falling, in a hush
He heard the ice-fields grind and crush.

His prow the sheeny south seas clove;
Warm, spiced winds from lemon grove
And heated thicket round him drove.

The storm-blast was his deity;
His lover was the fitful sea;
The wailing winds his melody.

By rocky scaur and beachy head
He followed where his fancy led,
And down the rainy waters fled;

And left the peopled towns behind,
And gave his days and nights to find
What lay beyond the western wind.

      —*L. Frank Tooker.*

Tacking Ship off Shore.

THE weather leech of the topsail shivers,
  The bowlines strain and the lee shrouds slacken;
The braces are taut and the lithe boom quivers,
  As the waves with the coming squall-cloud blacken.

Open one point on the weather bow,
  Is the light-house tall on Fire Island Head;
There's a shade of doubt on the Captain's brow,
  And the pilot watches the heaving lead.

I stand at the wheel, and with eager eye
  To sea and to sky, and to shore I gaze,
Till the muttered order of "Full and by"
  Is suddenly changed to "Full for stays."

The ship bends lower before the breeze,
  As her broadside fair to the blast she lays,
And she swifter springs to the rising seas
  As the pilot calls "Stand by for stays!"

It is silence all, as each in his place,
  With the gathered coil in his hardened hands,
By tack and bowline, by sheet and brace,
  Waiting the watchword, impatient stands.

And the light on Fire Island Head draws near,
  As trumpet-winged the pilot's shout
From his post on the bowsprit's heel I hear,
  With the welcome call of "Ready, about!"

No time to spare; 'tis touch and go,
    And the Captain growls, "Down helm! hard down!"
As my weight on the whirling spokes I throw,
While heaven grows black with the storm-clouds frown.

High o'er the knight-heads flies the spray,
    As we meet the shock of the plunging sea,
And my shoulder stiff to the wheel I lay,
    As I answer "Aye, aye, sir, hard a lee !"

With the swerving leap of a startled steed,
    The ship flies fast in the eye of the wind,
The dangerous shoals on the lee recede,
    And the headland white we have left behind.

The topsails flutter, the jibs collapse,
  And belly and tug at the groaning cleats;
The spanker slaps, and the mainsail flaps,
  And thunders the order, "Tacks and sheets!"

'Mid the rattle of blocks and the tramp of the crew,
  Hisses the rain of the rushing squall,
The sails are aback from clew to clew,
  And now is the moment for "Mainsail haul!"

And the heavy yards, like a baby's toy,
  By fifty strong arms are swiftly swung;
She holds her way, and I look with joy,
  For the first white spray o'er the bulwarks flung.

"Let go and haul!" 'tis the last command,
  And the head-sails fill to the blast once more,
Astern and to leeward lies the land,
  With its breakers white on the shingly shore.

What matters the reef or the rain or the squall,
  I steady the helm for the open sea;
The first mate clamors "Belay there all,"
  And the Captain's breath once more comes free.

And so off shore let the good ship fly,
  Little care I how the gusts may blow;
In my fo'castle bunk in a jacket dry,
  Eight bells have struck and my watch is below.

The Wife's Song.

SWING high and swing low while the breezes they
      blow,
It's off for a sailor thy father would go;
And it's here in the harbor in sight of the sea
He hath left his wee babe with my song and with me;
      "Swing high and swing low
      While the breezes they blow!"

Swing high and swing low while the breezes they blow!
It's oh for the waiting as weary days go!
And it's oh for the heartache that smiteth me when
I sing my song over and over again:
        "Swing high and swing low
        While the breezes they blow!"

"Swing high and swing low," the sea singeth so,
And it waileth anon in its ebb and its flow;
And a sleeper sleeps on to that song of the sea,
Nor recketh he ever of mine or of me!
        "Swing high and swing low
        While the breezes they blow,
    'Twas off for a sailor thy father would go!"

                        —*Eugene Field.*

"Oceanic" at Sea.

WHAT shall I sing of thee, my ship,
    Lone center of this orb of blue,
Horizoned by the rosy light
    Of peeping dawn, and sleeping evening too?

Thou art the pupil, ship of mine,
    Which lights this round and azure eye,
Rimmed by the rosy lids of dawn,
    And lost in sleep when evening rules the sky.

                        —*Charles A. Gunnison.*

The Ocean Wind.

The following little poem was written by the late Colonel E. D.
Baker, the celebrated orator and soldier, under interesting circum-
stances. Many years ago, before he had taken up arms in his country's service, he was walking home from church one Sunday with a
lady, who still resides in this city, when she complained of the buffet-
ing of the winds for which San Francisco was, and still is, famed. She
declared the wind to be the most unmannerly and prosaic thing in
nature, and at his remonstrance challenged him to say anything
poetic of it. The next morning she received the following verses and
note:

TO THE OCEAN WIND.

SEAWARD the mists lie dense and deep,
    And wild the tempests blow,
The sea-gull circles round the steep,
    And waves are white below.
Speed—speed—ye winds, your viewless flights,
    But landward as ye roam
Bear on your rustling wings to-night
    Health to her distant home.

Ye come from Isles of spice and bloom,
    Where palm trees line the strand,
Yet mingling with your rich perfume
    Airs from a colder land.
Loud tho' ye rage, and wild ye roar,
    Sweet is your breath, and free,
And full of blessings to the shore
    The storm that sweeps the sea.

But if those eddying blasts have power
    A wish or word to bear,
Seek ere ye sleep, my loved one's bower
    And leave my greeting there.
Whisper it gently in her ear
    When stars are in the sky,
And kiss away the starting tear
    When none but you are nigh.

Tell her I love her—in that word
    Soul, heart, thought, impulse thrill,
Tell her that every vow she heard
    I've fondly kept, and will.
Tell her—but, no, I soon shall see
    The "love light" in her eye.
Till then my only word shall be
    Love—blessing--and good-bye.

Mr. Baker presents his respectful compliments to Mrs. —— and sends the trifle enclosed as a proof (of which said proof she of all persons needs leastı that a lady's commands impel the commonest imagination into the forms of poetry even when the spirit is most wanting.

MONDAY MORNING.

The Derelict.

I AM the *Hakon Jarl.* The waters play
   Around my battered hull; and underneath
The sharks glide fishing. From the frozen North
The icebergs gather in a spectral fleet,
Shining in lakes of sea beneath the moon.

Drifting ! drifting ! Unto the misty port
Where neither signal-gun nor flashing wire
Sends back arrival to the anxious hearts,
That wander on the highlands and the shore.

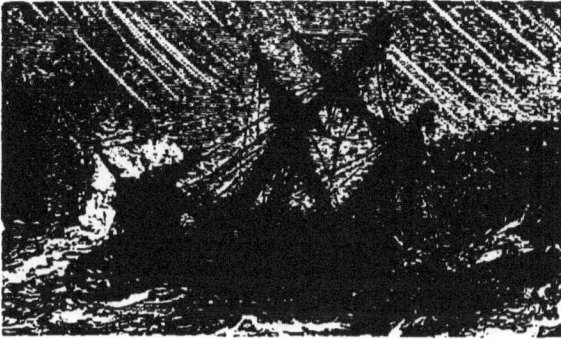

So shall ye drift, oh great, loud-clanging ships,
That pass me by, so haughty and so cold;
A mockery of death, a menace yet
To those that live and swim upon the sea.

And drifting ye shall follow all that were,
As all that are shall follow in their turn,
Until a light-house rises in the night,
From that dim port men call Oblivion.

—*John James Meehan.*

The Dreadnaught.

[The following ballad regarding the famous clipper Dreadnaught, was once the choice song of American sailors, and will bear printing.]

THERE'S a saucy wild packet, and a packet of
    fame,
She belongs to New York, and the Dreadnaught's
    her name.
She is bound to the westward where strong winds do
    blow,
Bound away in the Dreadnaught to the westward
    we go.

The time of her sailing is now drawing nigh;
Farewell pretty May, I must bid you good bye.
Farewell to old England and all there we hold dear,
Bound away in the Dreadnaught, to the westward
    we'll steer.

Oh, the Dreadnaught's hauling out of Waterloo dock,
Where the boys and the girls on the pier head do flock;
They will give us three cheers while their tears freely
    flow,
Saying, God bless the Dreadnaught whereso'er she
    may go.

Oh! the Dreadnaught is waiting in the Mersey so free,
Waiting for the Independence to tow her to sea;

For to round that black rock where the Mersey does
    flow.
Bound away in the Dreadnaught, to the westward
    we'll go.

Oh! the Dreadnaught's ahowling down the wild Irish
    shore,
Captain Samuels commands her as he's oft done
    before,
While the sailors like lions walk the decks to and fro,
Bound away in the Dreadnaught to the westward
    we'll go.

Oh! the Dreadnaught's a'sailing the Atlantic so wide,
Where the dark, heavy seas roll along the black side
With the sails neatly spread, and the red cross to show,
Bound away in the Dreadnaught to the westward
    we'll go.

Oh! the Dreadnaught's becalmed on the banks of
    Newfoundland,
Where the water's so green and the bottom is sand,
Where the fish of the ocean swim round to and fro,
Bound away in the Dreadnaught, to the westward
    we'll go.

Oh! the Dreadnaught's arrived in America once more,
We'll go ashore shipmates, on the land we adore,
See our wives and our sweethearts, be merry and free;
Drink a health to the Dreadnaught whereso'er she
    may be.

Here's a health to the Dreadnaught and to all her
      brave crew,
Here's health to Capt. Samuels and officers too,
Talk about your flash packets, "Swallow Tail" and
      "Black Ball,"
But the Dreadnaught's the clipper to beat one and all.

The Harbor of Dreams.

ONLY a whispering gale
    Flutters the wings of the boat;
Only a bird in the vale
Lends to the silence a note
Mellow, subdued, and remote;
This is the twilight of peace;
This is the hour of release;
Free of all worry and fret,
Clean of all care and regret,
When like a bird in its nest
Fancy lies folded to rest.
This is the margin of sleep;
Here let the anchor be cast;
Here in forgetfulness deep,

Now that the journey is past,
Lower the sails from the mast.
Here is the bay of content,
Heaven and earth interblent;
Here is the haven that lies
Close to the gates of surprise;
Here all like Paradise seems—
Here is the harbor of dreams.

—*F. D. Sherman.*

The Iron Ship.

"THE fabled seasnake, old Leviathan,
        Or else what grisly beast of scaly chine
That champed the oceanwrack, and swashed the brine
Before the new and milder days of man,
Had never rib nor bray nor swingeing fan
Like this iron swimmer of the Clyde or Tyne,
Late born of golden seed to breed a line
Of offspring swifter and more huge of plan.

"Straight is her going, for upon the sun
When once she hath looked, her path and place are
        plain;
With tireless speed she smiteth one by one
The shuddering seas and foams along the main;
And her eased breath when her wild race is run
Roars through her nostrils like a hurricane."

—*Robert Bridges.*

Reefing Topsails.

THREE hand-spike raps on the forward hatch,
   A hoarse voice shouts down the fo'castle dim,
Startling the sleeping starboard watch,
Out of their bunks, their clothes to snatch,
   With little thought of life or limb.

"All hands on deck! d'ye hear the news?
   Reef topsails all—'tis the old man's word.
Tumble up, never mind jackets or shoes!"
Never a man would dare refuse,
   When that stirring cry is heard.

The weather shrouds are like iron bars,
   The leeward backstays curving out.
Like steely spear-points gleam the stars
From the black sky flecked with feathery bars,
   By the storm-wind swerved about.

Across the bows like a sheeted ghost,
   Quivers a luminous cloud of spray,
Flooding the forward deck, and most
Of the waist; then, like a charging host,
   It rolls to leeward away.

"Mizzen topsail, clew up and furl;
   Clew up your main course now with a will !"
The wheel goes down with a sudden whirl.

"Ease her, ease her, the good old girl,
  Don't let your head sails fill !"

"Ease off lee braces; round in on the weather;
  Ease your halyards; clew down, clew down;
Haul out your reef tackles, now together."
Like an angry bull against his tether,
  Heave the folds of the topsails brown.

"Haul taut your buntlines, cheerly, men, now!"
  The gale sweeps down with a fiercer shriek;
Shock after shock on the weather bow
Thunders the head sea, and below
  Throbbing timbers groan and creak.

The topsail yards are down on the caps;
  Her head lies up in the eyes of the blast;
The bellying sails, with sudden slaps,
Swell out and angrily collapse,
  Shaking the head of the springing mast.

Wilder and heavier comes the gale
  Out of the heart of the Northern Sea;
And the phosphorescent gleamings pale
Surge up awash of the monkey rail
  Along our down pressed lee.

"Lay aloft ! lay aloft, boys, and reef,
  Don't let my starbolines be last,"
Cries from the deck the sturdy chief;
" 'Twill take a man of muscle and beef
  To get those ear-rings passed."

Into the rigging with a shout,
  Our second and third mates foremost spring;
Crackles the ice on the ratlines stout,
As the leaders on the yards lay out,
  And the footropes sway and swing.

On the weather end of the jumping yard,
  One hand on the lift, and one beneath,
Grasping the cringle, and tugging hard,
Black Dan, our third, grim and scarred,
  Clutches the ear-ring for life or death.

"Light up to windward," cries the mate,
  As he rides the surging yard arm end;
And into the work we threw our weight,
Every man bound to emulate,
  The rush of the gale, and the sea's wild send.

"Haul out to leeward," comes at last,
  With a cheering from the fore and main;
"Knot your reef-points, and knot them fast,"
Weather and lee are the ear-rings passed,
  And over the yard we bend and strain.

"Lay down men, all; and now with a will,
  Swing on your topsail halyards, and sway;
Ease your braces and let her fill,
There's an hour below of the mid-watch still,
  Haul taut your bowlines—well all—belay!"

                              — *Walter Mitchell.*

The Wind's Story.

THE North Wind blew at night off the sea,
　　Saying, "Sorrowful, sorrowful, all of me !
I sing of the numbing Winter's breath,
I sing of snow, and death.
I bring in the wave with the broken spar,
And the gray seas curling over the bar,
Drifting at night from a cold bright star—
　　Sorrowful, sorrowful, all of me !"

The South Wind blew at noon off the sea,
Singing, "Sorrowful, sorrowful, come to me !
I sing of the golden buttercup breath,
I sing the peace of death.
I bring in the shells with the laughing tide,
And follow the brown sails home, and slide
In the drowsy heat down the meadow side--
　　Sorrowful, sorrowful, come to me !"

The East Wind blew at morn off the sea,
Crying, "Sorrowful, sorrowful, all of me !
I sing of the piercing iceberg's breath,
I sing the horror of death.
And the tempest's shriek in the rigging black,
And the spindrift wreath and the rolling wrack,
And the boat that never again comes back—
　　Sorrowful, sorrowful, all of me !"

The West Wind blew at dawn off the sea,
Calling, "Sorrowful, sorrowful, come to me !
I sing of the joyous salt sea breath,
I sing, There is no death !
I murmur of sea caves rosy and deep,
And the glittering bay where the shoal fish leap,
And the lapse of the tide as it sinks to sleep—
Sorrowful, sorrowful, come to me !"

—*A. E. Gillington.*

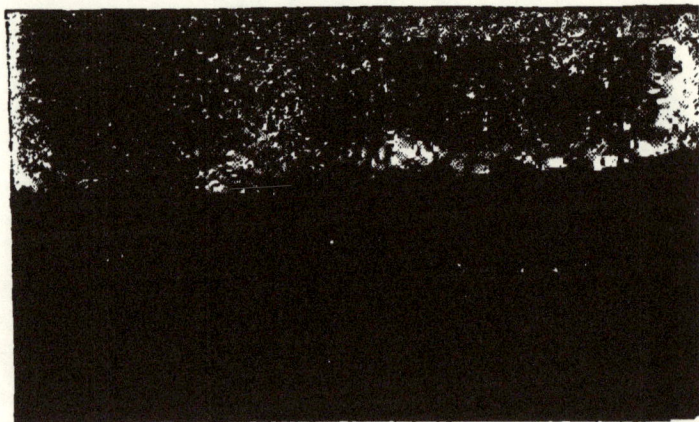

Gilbert 'a Becket.

THROUGH brawling Biscay to Ceuta's wave
   He has ridden unwrecked, our merchant brave;
But Gilbert à Becket, beware, beware !
For the sudden sail is the curs't Corsair.

They have rifled his silks and his good red gold,
And hurled him to rot in a dungeon hold ;
Till, Gilbert à Becket, for love of thee,
Thy jailer's daughter hath set thee free !

Starry eyes and a storm of hair,
And a voice like the wind harp on the air;
But, "Gilbert," "London," ere he goes,
All, all of his Northern speech she knows.

He has spun fresh silk, he has gotten fresh gold,
But his heart is behind in the Pirate's hold.
Now, Gilbert à Becket, what boots our wealth,
If a kanker lurks in our rose of health ?

Yet say, what burden of song is borne
Through thy open casement this summer morn ?
"Gilbert," "Gilbert," its accent rise,
"Gilbert," "Gilbert," despairing it dies.

Down the stair and into the street
He has flashed, his faithful love to meet.
Maid, in whose arms are thou folded fast ?
"Gilbert," "Gilbert," at last, at last!"

                    —Alfred Percival Graves

The Ships.

LOOK seaward, sentinel, and tell the land
What you behold.

SENTINEL.

I see the deep-plowed furrows of the main
  Bristling with harvest; funnel, and keel, and
    shroud,
  Heaving and hurrying hither through gale and
    cloud,
Winged by their burdens; argosies of grain,
Flocks of strange breed and herds of southern
  strain,
  Fantastic stuffs and fruits of tropic bloom,
Antarctic fleece and equatorial spice,
Cargoes of cotton, and flax, and silk and rice,
  Food for the hearth and staples for the loom;
Huge vats of sugar, cases of wine and oil,
  Summoned from every sea to one sole shore
  By Empire's scepter; the converging store
Of Trade's pacific universal spoil;
And heaving and hurrying hitherward to bring
  Tribute from every zone, they lift their voices,
  And as a strong man revels and rejoices,
They loudly and lustily chant, and this the song
  they sing:

CHORUS OF HOME–COMING SHIPS:

From the uttermost bound
  Of the wind and the foam,
From creek and from sound,
  We are hastening home.
We are laden with treasure
  From ransacked seas,
To charm your leisure
  To grace your ease.
We have trodden the billows,
  And tracked the ford,
To soften your pillows,
  To heap your board.
The hills have been shattered,
  The forests scattered,
Our white sails tattered,
  To swell your hoard.

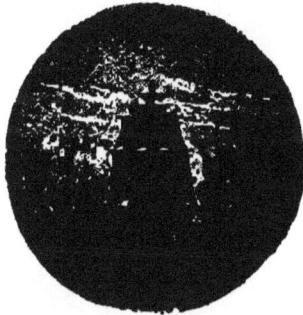

Is it blossom, or fruit, or
    Seed, you crave?
The land is your suitor,
    The sea your slave.
We have raced with the swallows,
    And threaded the floes
Where the walrus wallows
    'Mid melting snows;
Sought regions torrid
    And realms of sleet,
To gem your forehead,
    To swathe your feet,
And behold, now we tender,
    With pennons unfurled,
For your comfort and splendor,
    The wealth of the world.

                    —*Alfred Austin.*

The Sphynx of the Sea.

NOT to Egyptian sands alone belongs
    The storied Sphynx. Upon this mighty sea,
Her *alter ego* bides eternally,
And broods, inscrutable, o'er ancient wrongs.
Deaf to the magic of the mermaid's songs,
The minor music of the surge she hears;
The roar of Neptune; the wind's thousand tongues,
And shrieks of drowning men; yet guarded ears
Send up no message to the stony eyes
That stare across the waves in blank repose.
Though sun-kiss'd sails and dreary shipwrecks rise
And fall, by turns—dumbly she sits. She knows
Just where, in ocean's bed, the lost crew sleeps,
Yet, mutely cold, the Sphynx her secret keeps.

—*Eleanor C. Donnelly.*

Steamship Arabic.

WELCOME, old Arabic, again
    The ties which still do bind thee here
    Shall be, for many a coming year,
Thy truest, strongest anchor chain.

The flag thou bearest ne'er turns pale,
    The crimson flag which rules the wave,
    And God, who all that power gave,
Save thee from traitor, rock and gale.

I look with envy though and cry,
    "Would that the country of my birth
    Could claim a ship of equal worth,"
Proud then, by right, indeed were I.

And when I gaze at thy fair form,
    I pray that in the nearing time,
    Ships, fair as thee, in every clime
Beneath my flag shall brave the storm.

I pray some ship, as thee divine,
    Beneath my Stars and Stripes, may be
    Thy sister queen, and every sea
Shall know but thy loved flag and mine.

Now welcome to my home again,
    And to my arms and to my heart.
    Then when thy duty bids depart,
May fortune at thy helm remain.

           —*Charles A. Gunnison.*

The River.

I DREAMT dat I saw de ribber ob life,
 Dat flows to de Jaspah Sea,
De angels war wadin' to an' fro,
 But none ob 'em spoke to me.
Some dipped dere wings in de silv'ry tide;
Some were alone, and some side by side.
Nary a one dat I knew could I see
 In dat ribber ob life,
 De ribber ob life
Dat flows to de Jaspah Sea.

De ribber was wide, dat ribber ob life,
 De bottom I plainly could see;
De stones layin' dar was whiter den snow,
 De sands looked like gold to me.
But angels kep' wadin' to an' fro;
Whar did dey come f'om? Whar did dey go?
None ob 'em sinnahs like me, I know,
 In dat ribber ob life
 De ribber ob life
Dat flows to the Jaspah Sea.

De watch was clear as de "well by de gate,"
    Where Jesus de light first see,
De sof'est ob music f'om angel bands
Come ober dat ribber ob golden sands,
    Come ober dat ribber to me,
An' den I saw de clouds break way,
Revealin' de pearly gates ob day,
De beautiful day, dat nevah shall cease,
Whar all is joy, an' lub, and peace;
An, ovah dem gates was written so clear,
"Peace to all who entah here."
De angels was gedderin' 'round de frone,
De gate done close—I was left alone,
Alone on de banks ob a darken' stream;
But when I woke I foun' 'twas a dream.

I'se gwine to ford dat ribber ob life
    An' see eternal day;
I'se gwine to hear dem heabenly bands,
An' feel de tech ob ole-time hands,
    Dat long hab passed away.
Dars crowns ob glory fo' all, I'm told,
An' lubly harps wid strings ob gold;
An' I know ef dar's peace beyond dat sea,
Wid res' fo' de weary, dar's res' fo' me,
      Beyond dat ribber,
      Dat ribber ob life,
Dat flows to de Jaspah Sea.

The Skipper's Woes.

HAVE pity, ye Marine and Local Boards,
      Ye little magnates—yea, most mighty lords—
On the poor skipper, for his lot is cast
Where fate unkind pursues him to the last.
Alas! poor man, his, is an evil plight,
He's always wrong, he's never in the right.
Upon him, like a scapegoat, must be thrown
The faults of others, not to say his own;
Disaster comes, and tho' 'twas not his fault,
" 'Tis plain the fellow is not worth his salt."
Should fogs or currents put his reckoning out,
At once they ask, "What was the fool about ?"
His ship is wrecked, or by collision sunk;
Of course he has to prove he wasn't drunk.
If freights are low—who but himself to blame ?
Jack's duff is spoiled, at once he says the same;
The beef all bone and innocent of fat,
Who but the skipper is to blame for that ?
He shortens sail on some dark stormy night,
Jack growls and vows he did it out of spite.
Now he must teach the carpenter his trade;
Now show sailmaker how the sails are made.
In time of need he must be midwife too,
Or help to kill—as other doctors do.

Should a poor sailor sleep his last long sleep,
He—parson then—consigns him to the deep;
And if he has a tear or two to spare
He acts chief mourner, and bestows them there.
Well up in cooking, and in skill profound
At weighing tea and sugar by the pound;
Should there be strife or mutiny on board
He drops the scales and then takes up the sword.
And when the strife is over goes his rounds,
And—surgeon then—binds up the gaping wounds.
Now, an astronomer, he views the stars,
Measures a distance 'twixt the Moon and Mars;
A meteorologist we find him now,
Recording calms or winds—blow high or low.
Of course he's Euclid at his finger ends,
Or, what is harder, knows all knots and bends;
Is cunning, too, at mixing paints and oils,
Takes everthing in hand and nothing spoils.
Versed in exchanges—up in bills of lading,
And now a merchant, for his owners trading,
They praise him high, declare he is a gem;
The credit his—the cash all goes to them.
On deck all night amid the pelting rain,
In wearying calm or dreadful hurricane,
China typhoon, cyclone in Indian seas,
Afric's tornadoes—all mere trifles these;
Or a bright glare at night off Newfoundland,
Proclaims the dreaded iceberg close at hand.

[41]

Such danger's o'er, long-wished-for rest is sought,
But " Hard-a-starboard!" and then " Hard-a-port!"
Disturbs his dreams, and, rushing from below,
" A light close to, sir, on the weather bow!"
"Hard up!" bawls one; "Hard down!" another
    cries,
While half asleep the wearied skipper tries
To peer amid the gloom, there to discern
A steamer's light—now half a mile astern.
Once more he sleeps—but now his sleep evade
Dreams of Inquiry Courts and Boards of Trade.
On board a steamer now he scorns the wind,
But other cares oppress his anxious mind;
Of valves and pistons, cylinders and screws,
He knows, or ought to know, the names and use,
Surface condensers, steam and vacuum gauges.
Of coal combustion in its various stages,
Of salt in boilers and its incrustations,
Of screw propellers and side-wheel gyrations;
Of things in general—air, and sky, and sea—
A walking cyclopedia he must be.
Arrived in port.   " Well, what's up now," you ask.
They've found a little powder in a flask—
Fine him five pounds; and see—the careless dog—
Here's an omission in the official log;
Fine him again—the law must be enforced;
Some one must pay, so let him bear the cost;
Alas! poor skipper, if at sea you've trouble.

Arrived in port you may perhaps have double.
You're fined for this because you didn't do it.
For something else because you never knew it;
Fined to the last and turned from door to door
To find you are not wanted any more.

                              --*An Old Salt.*

Steamship Gaelic.

WITH steady, onward force she went
    From Orient to Occident.
The whistling winds which touched her shrouds,
Made music, while the evening clouds
Sweeping across the upper sea,
Sped not more gracefully than she.
Each foam-capped wave, which met her prow,
Kissed lightly as it were the brow
Of one he loved and worshiped too,
And then stood back for wondering view,
That one so graceful and so fair
Had hidden strength of whirlwind there.
Proudly she pressed, then spurned away
The clasping waves which longed to stay.
With freight of lives and silks and gold,
One hand alone her course controlled,
And she, consenting to obey,
Laughed at the storms by night and day;
Until, with well-earned praise elate,
She entered at the Golden Gate,
The Golden Gate of hate, of greed,
Of Mammon and his hungry breed,
Where bark the dogs which dare not bite,
Where clinking silver hushes right,
And for a time imprisoned lay
In the foul waters of the bay;

There chained, within the filthy tide,
Deep in her iron heart she cried,
"God let me float, forever blest,
Upon the Ocean's heaving breast,
Where winds untainted dash the spray
Upon my decks in boisterous play;
Where freedom means that one *is* free.
Grand, boundless, loved, unfathomed sea!
What joy to leave the sordid land,
To press the hollow of Thy hand."
The heavy anchors rose at last,
The colors floated from each mast;
Proudly disdainful, then she went
From Occident to Orient.

-Charles A. Gunnison.

The Mission of the Sea.

MEN gain new vigor at her wholesome breast;
  She links far lands and reunites fond hearts;
She carries argosies from East to West
    To those of distant parts.

But more than this her mission unto us,
    The mission of the many-voiced sea!
She rolls her ceaseless waves to shore, and thus
      She types Eternity.

[45]

Outward Bound.

ON the steady floor of earth there is solid ease an'
    mirth,
There's a wife, perhaps a sweetheart or a friend;
Through a roaring winter's night there's a lot o'
    warmth and light,
An' diversions fit to please you to the end.
In the blazin' of July to the 'ot an' achin' eye
There is meadows where the grass is wavin' green,
Through the streets a course you're trimmin' 'twixt a
    thousand pretty women,
Like flowers in the gardens to be seen.
        But a far, far voice is a-calling out to me,
        " Come away boy—away, with my billows
            for to be!"
        And my blood is beatin' briskly to the
            soundin' of the sea,
        And the " chantie " of the Outward Bound.

I landed from Rangoon just a year ago in June.
    And I thought the run was goin' to be my last;
An' 'ere once more am I in the middle of July,
    Lookin' out to sign agin afore the mast.
I'm a-weary of the land, though there's dollars to
    my hand,
    And I know I shall be dammin' in the boat;

But the wind is all off shore, in the city's loudest
    roar.
        There's a word passed along through the airs
           about the quays;
        " Round the world again let me send you
           swinging on my seas;
        On a big main-skys'l yarder with a slashin'
           tops'l breeze,
        Join the chorus of the Outward Bound! "

I was happy through that year, with my lovin' little
    dear,
And a rigger's berth ashore in Sunderland;
And I bet you'd never spot any neater little cot
Than the 'ome my little woman kept in hand.
But it lasted scarce as long as the singin' of a song,
And her face when last I kissed it was as ice;
And it's truth to you I tell, I'd as soon reside in hell
As the 'ouse that was my little paradise.
        So away once again on the round as never
           ends,
        With a fok's'le for my parlor, an' with Dutch-
           men for my friends—
        The only kind of 'ome as God A'mighty e'er
           intends
        For the comfort of the Outward Bound.

If you sailed at close of day, when the seas was
    cold an' gray,

An' the shore'ard lights were flyin' fast astarn,
When a takin' of your wheel, then some cur'us
things you'd feel,
An' a bit of "'Home an' England" you would
larn.
But be England far or nigh, it is all no odds to I,
By consequence of standin' quite alone;
So I twigs my compass card, an' I bites my chew of
"hard,"
While the shrouds is hummin' like a telephone.
"To her course hold her true, that's the
thing you've got to do;
All your friends and your relations is a cap-
tain an' a crew,
Till they slides you out o' soundin' an' you
sways in water blue,
Fathoms deep below the Outward Bound."

Then away my cares I'll fling when the decks they
are a-swing,
An' we're chuckin' all the Western ocean aft.
When we tumble to our places for to sweat the
blooming braces,
We'll sing a clipper's soul into the craft.
Though perhaps she is a witch and be'aves 'erself as
sich,
Slucin water on my blankets, bunk an' bed.
At the least she won't remind me of the foundered
'ome behind me,

And the gentle lass I laid among the dead.
>To its blazin' suns, an' bitter cold, an' roarin'
>>wind and weather,
>As'll tauten up my stays again, an' tan my
>>hide to leather.
>With Dagos, Dutch an' Englishmen a cursin'
>>all together
>In the fo'k'sle of the Outward Bound.

Evening Song to the Virgin.

AVE Sanctissima,
>We lift our souls to thee;
Ora pro nobis,
>Tis nightfall on the sea.
Watch us while shadows lie
>Far o'er the waters spread,
Hear the heart's lonely sigh,
>Thine too has bled.
Thou that has looked on Death,
>Aid us when Death is near,
Whisper of Heav'n to Faith,
>Sweet Mother, Sweet Mother hear!
Ora pro nobis,
>The wave must rock our sleep,
Ora Mater Ora, Star of the Deep.
>>>>>—*Mrs. Hemans.*

The Wreck of the Isle La Plante.

T'Was one dark night on Lac St. Pierre,
    De weend was blow, blow, blow,
W'en the crew of de wood skow Isle La Plante
    Got scare an' ron below.

For de weend she's blow lak horricane,
    Bimeby she blow some more,
W'en de skow buss up on Lac St Pierre,
    'Bout alf mile from de shore.

De captain, she's walk on de front deck,
    She's walk on de hin' deck too.
She's call de cook up from de hole,
    She's called hup all de crew.

De cook, he's name was Rosie,
  He's come from Montreal,
Was chambermaid hon lumber barge
  On de beeg Lachine canaul.

De weend, she's blow from de nor, eas, wes,
  De sou weend she's blow too,
W'en Rosie say, "Oh, Capitan,
  Wutever shall we do?"

De Captain, she's trow de hankre out,
  But still, de skow she's drift
For de crew, he can't pass on de shore
  Because he's loss de skeef.

De night was dark as one black cat,
  De wuve roa high and fass,
W'en de Captain take poor Rosie
  An' tie her by de mass.

Den de Captain, he's put on de life preserve,
  An' he jomp into de lake,
An' he say, "Good bye my Rosie, dear,
  I die for your sweet sake."

Nex morning very hearly,
  'Bout alf pass two, tree, four,
De Captain, cook an wood skow,
  Lay corpses on dat shore.

An de weend she's blow lak horricane,
  Bimeby she's blow some more,

An de skow buss up on Lac St. Pierre,
  'Bout alf mile from de shore.

L'ENVOI.

Now h'all good wood skow sailor mans
  Take warning by dat storm,
An go an marry one nice French girl
  And leeve on one good farm.

Den de weend she may blow lak horricane
  And spose she's blows some more,
You don't be drowned on Lac St. Pierre
  So longs you stop on shore.

The Ballad of the "Clamperdown."

IT was our war-ship Clamperdown,
   Would sweep the channel clean,
Wherefore she kept her hatches close
When the merry channel chops arose,
   To save the bleached marine.

There was one bow gun of a hundred ton,
   And a great stern gun beside;
They dipped their noses deep in the sea,
They racked their stays and stanchions free,
   In the wash of the wind-whipped tide.

It was our war-ship Clamperdown,
   Fell in with a cruiser tight,
That carried the dainty Hotchkiss gun
And a pair o' heels wherewith to run
   From the grip of a close-fought fight.

They opened fire at seven miles—
   As ye shoot at a bobbing cork—
And once they fired and twice they fired,
And the bow-gun drooped like a lily tired,
   That lolls upon the stalk.

"Captain, the bow-gun melts a pace,
   The deck-beams break below;
'Twere well to rest for an hour or twain,

And botch the shattered plates again,"
And he answered, "Make it so."

They opened fire within mile—
As ye shoot at the flying duck—
And the great stern-gun shot fair and true,
With the heave of the ship, to the stainless blue,
And the great stern-turret stuck.

"Captain, the turret fills with steam,
The feed-pipes burst below—
You can hear the hiss of the helpless ram,
You can hear the twisted runners jam,"
And he answered, "Turn and go!"

It was our war-ship Clamperdown,
And grimly did she roll;
Swung round to take the cruiser's fire
As the White Whale faces the Thresher's ire,
When they war by the frozen Pole.

"Captain, the shells are falling fast,
And faster still fall we;
And it is not meet for English stock
To wait, in the heart of an eight-day clock,
The death they can not see."

"Lie down, lie down, my bold A. B.,
We drift upon her beam;
We dare not ram, for she will run;
And dare ye fire another gun,
And die in the peeling steam?"

It was our war-ship Clamperdown
　　That bore an armor-belt;
But fifty feet at stern and bow
Lay bare as the paunch of the purser's sow,
　　To the hail of the Nordenfelt.

"Captain, they pierce the bow-plates through;
　　The chilled-steel bolts are swift!
We have emptied the bunkers in open sea,
Their shrapnel bursts where our coal should be."
　　And he answered, "Let her drift."

It was our war-ship Clamperdown,
　　Swung round upon the tide.
Her two dumb guns glared south and north,
And the blood and the bubbling steam ran forth,
　　And she ground the cruiser's side.

"Captain, they cry the fight is done;
They bid you send your sword."
And he anwered, "Grapple her stern and bow.
They have asked for the steel.　They shall have it
　　　　now;
　　Out cutlasses and board!"

It was our war-ship Clamperdown,
　　Spewed up four hundred men;
And the scalded stokers yelped delight,
As they rolled in the waist and heard the fight,
　　Rave over their steel-walled pen.

They cleared the cruiser end to end,
    From conning-tower to hold.
They fought as they fought in Nelson's fleet;
They were stripped to the waist, they were bare of
        the feet,
    As it was in the days of old.

It was the sinking Clamperdown
    Heaved up her battered side—
And carried a million pounds in steel,
To the cod and the corpse-fed conger-eel,
    And the scour of the Channel tide.

It was the crew of the Clamperdown
    Stood out to sweep the sea,
On a cruiser won from an ancient foe,
As it was in the days of long ago,
    And as it still shall be.

(Kipling)

APPENDIX.

Appendix.

"Si monumentum quaeris circumspice."

Maritime melodies are behind you, Chanties, and an omnium gatherum before you. When the COM-MERCIAL PUBLISHING COMPANY decided on this book as a Christmas souvenir to its best friends, the compiler was given *carte blanche* in the matter. With a ten-derness for some poems not maritime, and having in them no reference to the business office of this com-pany, he decided to sandwich them between the little gems of a business character, hoping the reader will be led on to the end of the book, and that the business maxims it teaches, while impressing each one, will be brightened by the selections that have no reference to the printer's craft. The COMMERCIAL PUBLISHING COMPANY has to thank many friends for contributions to these pages, which are made up from poems clipped from exchanges chiefly, and credit is in each case given to the author where known, but in no case to the paper from which it was taken, as nearly all have been passed along from one journal to another by the omnivorous scissors editor.

The poems unsigned are, therefore, from the pen of one unknown to this office or one too modest to become famous in this book.

✳ ✳ Chanties ✳ ✳

IT WAS the intention to give in this edition of "Maritime Melodies" a number of chanties, but without the music, the action and the very spirit of the sea, words are feeble.

The "Chanty," a corruption of the French verb to sing, came from New Orleans, where the French darkies made up songs to suit the occasion as they loaded the Yankee clipper ships with cotton. The Yankee sailor in turn "caught on" and calling their songs "Shanties," made rhymes and fitted them to music that assisted in heaving anchor, setting and furling sails, pumping out the ship, etc. And now the "motif" is explained.

With the decadence of the American marine since "the late unpleasantness" between the brethren North and South, who, before and since that episode have dwelt together in unity, it has been an unfortunate fact that the American Mercantile Marine is more of a theory than a condition. With the ship, the American sailor has also disappeared. But the Shanty remains. Listen. The fine 100 A1 British ship California, a good ship with a good name, but flying the flag of Great Britain, instead of the Stars and Stripes, officered and manned by lusty Britons, good fellows all, but unfortunate in not being born here: The fine ship California is leaving the State

for which she is named, and on the order to heave up
anchor, the Chanty man starts in:

"As I was walking down the street,
 Hoodah, to my Hoodah;
A charming girl I chanced to meet,.
 Hoodah, Hoodah day.

———

Blow ye winds, heigho,
 For California, O;
There's plenty of gold
 So I've been told
On the banks of Sacramento.

"ON THE BANKS OF SACRAMENTO."

While there is much about the Yankee skipper,
the Yankee clipper, the famous Black Ball line, in
every chanty sung aboard any ship, American or for-

eign, the only collection of Chanties is an English edition in which these references are generally eliminated, while as sung aboard ship, there is so much that while forcible is hardly polite, it is impossible to reprint those particular chanties having reference to the past glories of American shipping. Therefore Chanties cut no further figure in this book, but songs with the sea for their subject are again used in MARITIME MELODIES.

yy Merchants.

THERE'S many a merchant who is yy
  Enough to take his ee.
To study business with his ii
  COMMERCIAL NEWS he cc.

This valued journal he will uu,
  Lest trade with him dk
No clerk of his will he xqq
  Who reads it not each day.

Result is, he but little oo,
  Has much with which to pay.
This hint you'll take, unless u r
  What some folks call a j.

The Rhyme of the Printer.

CALKERS and shipwrights,
  Also midshipmites,
'Prentice and captains,
Builders of capstans,
While all jolly tars,
The makers of spars,
Liners and brokers,
Coal dusty stokers,
Runner and agent,
Make up the pageant,
With sellers of wheat
And dealers in meat,
Exporters of wares,
The brokers in fares,
Owners of whalers,
Steamers and sailers
Of iron or wood;
The dealers in food;
These also and more
Crowd up at the door
Where eagle o'erhead
(No pinions are spread)
Sits there evermore
Above **34**.

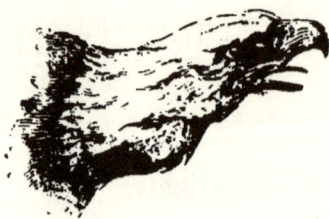

Now cannot you see
And with me agree
That this **34**
Is over the door
Through which you must go
For printing, you know,
For ledgers and bills,
Newspapers or wills,
For charters or cards,
Or posters by yards.
No need to say more,
Just try **34**.

      Commercial Publishing Co.,
          Printers and Publishers,
            34 California street,
          Sign of the Eagle's Head.

The Bachelor.

HE does not choose a single flower
  And look at that alone;
He does not praise two twinkling stars
  As if no others shown.

Though liking beef yet he likes quail,
  Two very different things;
And need it follow he hates ale
  Because champagne he sings?

Blue eyes he loves, and he loves gray,
  While black seem just as fair,
And he may praise on any day
  Both brown and golden hair.

Thus sing he may all shades of red,
  And tresses bleached or blue,
E'en worship some false-fronted head
  And yet to all be true.

But surely some sad fate awaits,
  (Far worse than Adam's fall,)
The man who will not take a half
  Because he can't get all.
                    —*Charles A. Gunnison.*

Complete Resignation.

HE left his club, he gave up smoking,
    At night dared not out doors to stir;
At last through her demands provoking,
    No more was left—he gave up her.
And subscribed for the COMMERCIAL NEWS, as be-
ing better, cheaper and more companionable.

Ye Bonanza

THE STORY OF A NEW AND SEDUCTIVE DRINK.

IT was a gallant stranger,
    Of goodly height and weight,
Who wore a bale of whiskers
Most fierce to contemplate,
An eke an air of freshness
Brought from ye Golden Gate.

He came into my sanctum
One pleasant afternoon,
And hinted that we visit
Some neighboring saloon;
I made a bad exception
And went with him full soon.

When we arrived, ye stranger,
Who hailed from ye coast,
Drew forth a yellow eagle,
And shouted to mine host:
"Ho! mix us two bonanzas,
We fain would drink a toast!"

Then did ye skillful mixer
Two bottles set in line,
Ye one contained brandy,
Ye other yellow wine,
And these two pleasant liquids
Proceeded to combine.

Ye stranger eyed ye compound
With sigh of deepest bliss;
Then down his hairy gullet
It slipped with gurgling hiss,
And I did cast a bumper
Into mine own abyss.

Then forth again we sallied
Into ye outer air,
When lo! this world seemed glorious,
This life a boon most rare,
And that bewhiskered giant
A man divinely fair!

Quoth I: "This same bonanza
Puts fire into ye heart.

Return with me, I prithe,
Unto ye liquor mart,
And I, as doth beseem me,
Will play ye buyer's part."

When next again we sallied
Into ye crowded street,
'Twas arm in arm we wandered
And lifted high our feet,
Ye while ye gracious pavement
Rose up our souls to meet.

Ye third time that we issued
From that accursed den
A change was wrought within us,
Defying tongue or pen.
Each fireplug seem'd a hogshead,
Each man looked like to ten.

And still a fourth bonanza
Each poured into his face,
Which caused ye mighty buildings
All round about to chase,
And made ye streets and alleys
Tie up and interlace.

Anon ye swaying sidewalk
Grew rife with wriggling things;
With lobsters, pterodactyls,
And toads with fiery wings,

With blue and greenish devils,
And snakes with twisting stings.

That night within ye prison
I slept as sleep ye dead;
My right arm for a pillow,
An oak plank for a bed;
And when I woke ye morrow,
I wondered at my head!

Since then within my pocket
I bear a monstrous gun;
Perchance I may encounter
Again that Native Son;
And if he says "bonanza"
I'll either shoot or run!

— *George Horton.*

Found.

L ITTLE Bo Peep, she lost her sheep,
But knew just how to find 'em;
An "ad" in this paper*
Brought the sheep with a caper,
And a bill tied on behind 'em.

[*"This paper," of course, refers to the COMMERCIAL
NEWS, although there is no copyright on the above
beautiful poem.]

[69]

The Ruling Hand.

I HAVE read in song and story
   Of the honest hand of toil;
Of the strong right hand of labor
   And the hand that tills the soil.
I have heard the sweet old saying,
   In the dust of ages furled,
That the hand that rocks the cradle
   Is the hand that rules the world.

I have harkened to the singing,
   And have wondered at the song;
For I deem the theme poetic,
   Though I hold the legend wrong.
Not the hand that rocks the cradle,
   Nor the babe's rose-palm up-curled,
Is the hand that sways the nations
   And the hand that rules the world.

Speak not of the hand of guidance,
   Pointing out the narrow way,
For the royal hand I sing of
   Is a mightier one than they;
Than the hand that bears the banner
   Through the smoke of battle hurled,
For the great hand is the straight hand
   And the hand that rules the world

Tell me not of hands heroic,
   Battling for our fellow men;
Of the helping hand of woman,
   Or the hand that wields the pen;
Nor the hand that beats the carpet
   On the back-yard fence unfurled;
For the hand that beats four aces
   Is the hand that rules the world.

                    —*Kate Masterson.*

Came to the Right Shop.

THERE was a man in our town,
   And he was wondrous wise,
He came into our printing house
   Because we advertise.

And when he found our model shop
   He quickly did explain
He wanted lots of printing done,
   Some fancy, other plain.

To Rudyard Kipling

ON HIS FINDING THE PROPER SPOT ON WHICH TO CHASTISE U. S.

YOU'RE a dandy, you're a daisy
    Rudyard, were I not so lazy
I would write in elegiacs
Four score thousand lines of praise.
Thank your stars I was born tired;
Though my soul by song is fired
I am far too weary, Rudyard,
For to fan it to a blaze.

But I love you for your muscle,
And the never-ending bustle
You've kicked up in one short journey
Through our "God Almighty" land,
By the much-deserved, sharp spanking
You have given us, and thanking
You for all those stories stolen,
Compliment you on your sand.

Glad you knocked Chicago silly,
She deserved it, rampant filly,
Saying that she heads this nation;
But you found her place of rank,
Though our land be fair as Venus,
(Here's a little joke between us),
She's the middle of the country,
And the proper place to spank!

                    —*Charles A. Gunnison.*

[72]

Gladstone's Mistake.

Here is a test which is used among English school boys as "Peter Piper picked a peck of pickled peppers" is used in this country. It is a catch in writing, as well as in speaking, and is attributed to Gladstone:

WHILE hewing yews, Hew lost his ewe,
    And put it in the "Hue and Cry."
To name its face's dusky hues
Was all the effort he could use.
You brought it to him by-and-by
And only asked the hewer's ewer,
Your hands to wash in water pure,
Lest nice-nosed ladies not a few
Should cry on coming near you, "Ugh!"

The "Hue and Cry was not the press,
As we can show, and want redress.

You brought the ewe back from the news,
The NEWS contained (which you peruse)
The ewe belonged to Hugh's mews.
He gave you pesos dos Peru's
Or Hugh's silver gained from ewes,
Or else from yews, which Hugh now hews,
The silver came.   A part you use
In purchase of

                COMMERCIAL NEWS.

The Bottle and the Bird.

ONCE on a time a friend of mine prevailed on
    me to go
To see the dazzling splendors of a sinful ballet show,
And after we had reveled in the salatory sights,
We sought a neighboring café for more tangible
    delights;
When I demanded of my friend what viands he
    preferred,
He quoth: "A large cold bottle and small hot
    bird!"

Fool that I was, I did not know what anguish hidden
    lies
Within the morceau that allures the nostrils and the
    eyes!
There is a glorious candor in an honest quart of
    wine—
A certain inspiration which I cannot well define!
How it bubbles, how it sparkles, how its gurgling
    seems to say:
"Come, on a tide of rapture let me float your soul
    away!"

But the crispy steaming mouthful that is spread upon
    your plate—
How it discounts human sapience and satirizes fate!

You wouldn't think a thing so small could cause
    the pains and aches
That certainly accrue to him that of that thing
    partakes;
To me, at least (a guileless wight!), it never once
    occurred
What horror was encompassed in that small hot
    bird.

Oh, what a head I had on me when I awoke next
    day,
And what a firm conviction of intestinal decay!
What seas of mineral water and of bromide I ap-
    plied
To quench those fierce volcanic fires that rioted
    inside!
And, oh! the thousand solemn, awful vows I plighted
    then
Never to tax my system with a small hot bird again!

The doctor seemed to doubt that birds could worry
    people so,
But, bless him! since I ate the bird, I guess I ought
    to know!
The acidous condition of my stomach, so he said,
Bespoke a vinous irritant that amplified my head,
And, ergo, the causation of the thing, as he inferred,
Was the large cold bottle, *not* the small hot bird.

Of course I know it wasn't, and I'm sure you'll say
I'm right
If ever it has been your wont to train around at
night;
How sweet is retrospection when one's heart is
bathed in wine,
And before its balmy breath how do the ills of life
decline!
How the gracious juices drown what grief would vex
a mortal breast,
And float the flattered soul into the port of dreamless
rest!

But you, O noxious pigmy bird! whether it be you
fly
Or paddle in the stagnant pools that sweltering,
festering lie—
I curse you and your evil kind for that you do me
wrong,
Engendering poisons that corrupt my petted muse of
song;
Go, get thee hence, and never more discomfort me
and mine—
I fain would barter all thy brood for one sweet
draught of wine!

So, hither come, O sportive youth! when fades the
tell-tale day—

Come hither with your fillets and your wreaths of
     posies gay;
We shall unloose the fragrant seas of seething, froth-
     ing wine
Which now the cobwebbed glass and envious wire
     and corks confine,
And midst the pleasing revelry the praises shall be
     heard
Of the large cold bottle, *not* the small hot bird!

                         —Eugene Field.

A Good Investment.

THERE was a young man of La Rue's,
Who constantly studied the NEWS.
In less than a year
He had nothing to fear,
As he had a large fortune to use.

Feeling proud of his very great hoard,
He purchased a seat in the Board;
He paid such a price,
(Although t'was not nice),
He gave up the NEWS he adored.

Attempting to shorten some wheat,
(Considered a dangerous feat),
At the end of a year
To all it was clear
He had lost both his money and seat.

He purchased the NEWS at this time,
Having borrowed the half of a dime.
With this fund of knowledge,
As though fresh from college,
He acted with courage sublime.

Out of charters he made a great pile,
Which frequently caused him to smile,

And he said "it is plain,
My losses in grain
Came from stopping the NEWS for a while."

So now this young man from La Rue's
Not only subscribes for the NEWS,
But he orders each day,
In the NEWS (with display),
An "ad" for his friends to peruse.

www.ingramcontent.com/pod-product-compliance
Lightning Source LLC
Chambersburg PA
CBHW022143090426
42742CB00010B/1371

* 9 7 8 3 7 4 4 7 9 7 4 5 0 *